What Every Teacher Should Know About Educational Assessment

W. James Popham
University of California, Los Angeles

Boston   New York   San Francisco
Mexico City   Montreal   Toronto   London   Madrid   Munich   Paris
Hong Kong   Singapore   Tokyo   Cape Town   Sydney

TABLE OF CONTENTS

What Every Teacher Should Know About Educational Assessment

1: What Do Teachers Need to Know About Assessment

In this first section, the emphasis is on why teachers need to know about assessment. Educational assessment is defined as a formal attempt to determine students' status with respect to educational variables of interest. Based on teachers' classroom activities, there are four traditional reasons why teachers assess—namely, to (1) diagnose students' strengths and weaknesses, (2) monitor students' progress, (3) assign grades, and (4) determine the teacher's instructional effectiveness. Based on recent uses of educational assessment results, three more current reasons that teachers need to know about instruction can be identified. Those more recent functions of educational tests are to (1) influence public perceptions of educational effectiveness, (2) help evaluate teachers, and (3) clarify teachers' instructional intentions. Regardless of the specific application of test results, however, teachers should use the results of assessments to make better decisions. That's really the only excuse for taking up students' time with assessment.

Whether you are already a teacher or are preparing to become a teacher, you really do need to know about educational assessment. But the field of educational assessment contains huge chunks of information. In fact, some educators devote their entire careers to assessment. Clearly, there's more to educational assessment than you probably care to know. The question is, What should classroom teachers know about assessment?

The title of this booklet suggests an answer—namely, *What Every Teacher Should Know about Classroom Assessment*. The key word in the title, at least for purposes of this discussion, is *should*. There are oodles of fascinating things about assessment that you might learn. You'd even find a few of them interesting (not all that many, I suspect). But to help your students learn, you really don't need to know a host of assessment esoterica. This booklet about educational assessment is deliberately focused on only those things that you really must know in order to promote your students' learning most effectively. I am altogether reluctant to clutter your head with a galaxy of nice-to-know but nonessential knowledge about educational assessment. Such nice-to-know content often crowds out the need-to-know content. There is, after all, only so much skull space available.

It may be easier for you to get a handle on what you'll be reading if you realize you'll be covering topics that deal chiefly with:

1.   Constructing your own assessment instruments
2.   Using assessment instruments constructed by others
3.   Planning instruction based on instructionally illuminating assessments

Good luck in taking this brief dip into the classroom assessment pool!

2: Reliability

This section focuses on the reliability of educational assessment procedures. Reliability refers to the consistency with which a test measures whatever it's measuring—that is, the absence of measurement errors that would distort an examinee's score.

There are three distinct types of reliability evidence. *Stability reliability* refers to the consistency of examinees' scores over time. Stability reliability is usually represented by a test-retest coefficient of correlation between examinees' scores on two occasions, but can be indicated by the degree of classification consistency displayed for examinees on two measurement occasions. *Alternate-form reliability* refers to the consistency of results between two or more forms of the same test. Alternate-form reliability is usually represented by the correlation of examinees' scores on two different test forms, but can also be reflected by classification-consistency percentages. *Internal consistency* represents the degree of homogeneity in an assessment procedure's items. Common indices of internal consistency are the Kuder-Richardson formulae as well as Cronbach's coefficient *alpha*. The three forms of reliability evidence should *not* be used interchangeably, but should be sought for the educational purpose to which an assessment procedure is being put—that is, the kind of educational decision linked to the assessment's results.

The standard error of measurement supplies an indication of the consistency of an individual's score by estimating person-score consistency from evidence of group-score consistency. The standard error of measurement is interpreted in a manner similar to the plus or minus sampling-error estimates often provided with national surveys. Classroom teachers are advised to become generally familiar with the key notions of reliability, but not to subject their own classroom tests to reliability analyses unless the tests are unusually important.

What do you, as a teacher or teacher in preparation, truly need to know about reliability? Do you, for example, need to gather data from your own classroom assessment procedures so you can actually calculate reliability coefficients? If so, do you need to collect all three varieties of reliability evidence? My answers may surprise you. I think you need to know what reliability is, but I don't think you'll have much call to use it with your own tests—you won't, that is, unless certain of your tests are extraordinarily significant. And I haven't run into classroom tests, even rocko-socko final examinations, that I would consider sufficiently significant to warrant your whipping up a reliability extravaganza. In general, if you construct your own classroom tests with care, those tests will be sufficiently reliable for the decisions you will base on the tests' results.

You need to know about what reliability is because you may be called on to explain to parents the meaning of a student's standardized test scores, and you'll want to know how reliable the test is. You need to know what the test manual's authors are talking about and to be wary of those who secure one type of reliability evidence—for instance, a form of internal consistency evidence (because it's the easiest to obtain)—then try to proclaim that form of reliability evidence provides an indication of the test's stability or the comparability of its multiple forms. In short, you need to be at least knowledgeable about the fundamental meaning of reliability, but I do not suggest you make your own classroom tests pass any sort of reliability muster.

Reliability is a central concept in measurement. As you'll see in the next section, if an assessment procedure fails to yield consistent results, it is almost impossible to make any accurate inferences about what a student's score signifies. Inconsistent measurement is, at least some of the time, bound to be inaccurate measurement. Thus, you should realize that as the stakes associated with an assessment procedure become higher, there will typically be more attention given to establishing that the assessment procedure is, indeed, reliable. If you're evaluating an important test developed by others and you see that only skimpy attention has been given to the establishment of reliability, you should be critical of the test because evidence regarding an essential attribute of an educational test is missing.

The other thing that you should know about reliability is that it comes in three brands—three kinds of evidence about a test's consistency that are not interchangeable. Don't let someone foist a set of internal consistency results on you and suggest that these results tell you anything of importance about stability. Don't let anyone tell you that a stability reliability coefficient indicates anything about the equivalence of a test's multiple forms. Although the three types of reliability evidence are related, they really are fairly distinctive kinds of creatures, something along the lines of second or third cousins.

What I'm trying to suggest is that classroom teachers, as professionals in the field of education, need to understand that an important attribute of educational assessment procedures is reliability. The higher the stakes associated with a test's use, the more the educators should attend to the assessment procedure's reliability. Reliability is such a key criterion by which psychometricians evaluate tests that you really ought to know what it is, even if you don't use it on a daily basis.

The situation regarding your knowledge about reliability is somewhat analogous to a health professional's knowledge about blood pressure and how blood pressure influences one's health. Even though only a small proportion of health professionals work directly with patients' blood pressure on a day-by-day basis, there are few health professionals who don't know at least the fundamentals of how one's blood pressure can influence a person's health. Although I don't think you should devote any time to calculating the reliability of your own classroom tests, I think you should have a general knowledge about what it is and why it's important. Besides, computing too many reliability coefficients for your own classroom tests might give you high blood pressure.

3

3: Validity

Validity, in educational assessment, refers to the accuracy of an inference about a student's unseen status (for instance, the student's ability to spell) based on the student's assessed performance (for instance, the student's score on a spelling test). There are three forms of validity evidence that can be used to support validity. Content-related evidence provides a picture of the extent to which an assessment procedure suitably samples the content of the assessment domain it represents. Criterion-related evidence of validity deals with the degree to which an exam accurately predicts a student's subsequent status. Construct-related evidence of validity deals with the assembly of empirical evidence that a hypothetical construct, such as a student's ability to generate written compositions, is accurately assessed.

The relationship between validity evidence and reliability evidence should be considered, as should certain unsanctioned forms of validity. In general, more validity evidence is better than less, but that classroom teachers need to be realistic in how much evidence of validity to secure for their own tests. I recommend teachers become familiar with all three forms of evidence, but to focus only on content-related evidence of validity for their own classroom assessment procedures.

How much, if anything, do classroom teachers really need to know about validity? Do classroom teachers need to collect validity evidence for their own tests? If so, what kind(s)?

As with reliability, I think a classroom teacher needs to understand what the essential nature of the three kinds of validity evidence is, but I don't think that classroom teachers need to go into a frenzy of evidence gathering regarding validity. Clearly, if you're a teacher or a teacher in preparation, you'll be far too busy in your classroom trying to keep ahead of the students to spend much time in assembling validity evidence. I do recommend, however, that for your more important tests, you devote at least some attention to content-related evidence of validity. I suggest giving serious thought to the content of an assessment domain being represented by a test is a good first step. Having a colleague review your tests' content is also an effective way to help make sure that your classroom tests represent satisfactorily the content you're trying to promote, and that your score-based inferences about your students' status are not miles off the mark.

Regarding the other two forms of validity evidence, however, I urge little more than a reasonable understanding of what those kinds of evidence are like. If you're ever asked to help scrutinize a high-stakes educational test, you'll want to know enough about such versions of validity evidence so that you're not intimidated when measurement specialists start reciting their "odes to validity."

4: Absence-of-Bias

This section on absence-of-bias is, quite naturally, focused on how educators make bias absent. Assessment bias is any element in an assessment procedure that offends or unfairly penalizes students because of personal characteristics, such as their gender and ethnicity. Assessment bias, when present, was seen to distort certain students' performances on educational tests, hence reduce the validity of score-based inferences about those students. The two chief contributors to assessment bias are offensiveness and unfair penalization. An examination having a disparate impact on a particular subgroup is not necessarily biased, although such a differential impact certainly would warrant further scrutiny of the examination's content to discern if assessment bias was present. In many instances, disparate impact from an examination simply indicates that certain groups of students have previously received inadequate instruction.

There are two procedures for identifying biased segments of educational assessment devices. A judgmental approach relies on the considered opinions of properly oriented bias reviewers. Judgmental approaches to bias detection can be formally employed with high-stakes tests or less formally used by classroom teachers. An empirical approach that relies chiefly on differential item functioning can also be used, although its application requires large numbers of students. I recommend that classroom teachers be vigilant in the identification of bias, whether in their own tests or in the tests of others. For detecting bias in their own tests, classroom teachers are urged to adopt a judgmental review strategy consonant with the importance of the assessment procedures being involved.

There are issues associated with the assessment of students with limited-English proficiency and students who are disabled. In some cases, assessment accommodations can yield more valid inferences about students with disabilities or less conversance with English. In other instances, alternate assessments need to be developed. Neither of these assessment alterations, however, is completely satisfactory in coping with this important assessment issue.

Classroom teachers need to know that assessment bias exists. Assessment bias in educational tests is probably less prevalent than it was a decade or two ago because most measurement specialists, after having been sensitized to the presence of assessment bias, now strive to eliminate such biases. However, for the kinds of teacher-developed assessment procedures seen in typical classrooms, systematic attention to bias eradication is much less common.

All classroom teachers *routinely* need to use absence-of-bias as one of the three evaluative criteria by which they judge their own assessments and those educational assessments developed by others. For instance, if you are ever called on to review the quality of a high-stakes test such as a district-developed or district-adopted examination whose results will have a meaningful impact on students' lives, be sure that suitable absence-of-bias procedures, both judgmental and empirical, were employed during the examination's development.

But what about your own tests? How much effort should you devote to making sure that your tests don't offend or unfairly penalize any of your students because of personal characteristics such as ethnicity or gender? My answer is that you really do need to devote attention to absence-of-bias for *all* of your classroom assessment procedures. For the least significant of your assessment procedures, I suggest that you simply heighten your consciousness about bias eradication as you generate the test items or, having done so, as you review the completed test.

For more important examinations, try to enlist the assistance of a colleague to review your assessment instruments. If possible, attempt to secure the help of colleagues from the same subgroups as those represented in your students. For instance, if many of your students are Hispanics (and you aren't), then try to get an Hispanic colleague to look over your test's items to see if there are any that might offend or unfairly penalize Hispanic students. When you enlist colleagues to help you review your tests for potential bias, briefly describe to your co-workers how you define assessment bias, give them a succinct orientation to the review task, and structure their reviews with absence-of-bias questions regarding offensiveness and unfair penalization.

Most importantly, if you personally realize how repugnant all forms of assessment bias are, and how it can distort certain students' performances even if the assessment bias was inadvertently introduced by the test's developer, you'll be far more likely to eliminate assessment bias in your own tests. In education, as in any other field, assessment bias should definitely be *absent*.

5: What to Assess and How to Assess It

Two major questions guided the content of this section—namely, what should a classroom teacher assess and, having answered that question, how should it be assessed? I contend that both of these decisions must be primarily influenced by the decisions that the teacher hopes to illuminate by gathering assessment data from students.

In determining what to assess, instructional objectives can play a prominent role in the teacher's choice of assessment emphases. In particular, broad-scope measurable objectives are recommended as helpful vehicles for identifying potential assessment targets. The three domains of student outcomes contained in Bloom's *Taxonomies of Educational Objectives* are a helpful framework to decide whether there are instructional and assessment overemphases on cognitive outcomes and, if so, whether too much instruction and assessment attention are being given to the lowest level of that taxonomy. Three other recommended considerations when teachers set out to answer the what-to-assess question are (1) the content standards recommended by national organizations, (2) the NAEP assessment frameworks, and (3) the views of colleagues.

What is the main message of this section for classroom teachers who must decide what to assess and how to assess it? The answer is rather straightforward. All you need to do is to think seriously about both questions. Any experienced teacher will, if pressed, confess that instructional inertia plays a key role in what usually goes on in the teacher's classroom. Classroom teachers find it far easier to engage in activities this year than they engaged in last year simply because it takes less effort to employ "same-old, same-old" instructional procedures than to install new instructional procedures. There's also assessment inertia that inclines teachers to rely on whatever assessment schemes they've previously utilized. It's so much simpler to massage last year's true-false exams than to whip out a brand new performance test.

In recognition of these all-too-human tendencies to adopt the path of least resistance, it becomes more important to try to "get it right the first time" or, putting it in more pedantic parlance, to "eschew egregiously inferior initial assessment conceptualizations." In other words, the more up-front thought that teachers give to answering the what-to-assess and how-to-assess-it questions, the more likely they'll be to avoid the kind of serious assessment errors that, because of practical pressures, may plague them for years.

You really do need to acquire some familiarity with the three taxonomic domains. Many educators pepper their language with references to cognitive, psychomotor, or affective educational outcomes. Just so you don't look like a ninny at faculty meetings when folks use such terms, a little knowledge about the three domains will prove useful. (And knowledge, of course, is only at the lowest level of the cognitive domain.)

You also need to know that a small number of broad-scope instructional objectives can prove useful to you in deciding what to assess, but that a litany of small-scope objectives won't help you much in your instruction or your assessment because you're apt to be overwhelmed by them. And a review of documents containing relevant content standards is almost always going to be of some help to you. Most importantly, however, is the idea that you need to devote serious up-front thought to the decisions that you want your classroom assessment to inform, then assess your students in accord with those decision options.

6: Selected-Response Items

As you can discern from this section's title, it's going to describe how to construct selected-response kinds of test items. You'll learn how to create four different varieties of selected-response test items—namely, binary-choice items, multiple binary-choice items, multiple-choice items, and matching items. All four of these selected-response kinds of items can be used effectively by teachers to derive defensible inferences about students' cognitive status—that is, the knowledge and skills that teachers typically try to promote in their students.

But no matter whether you're developing selected-response or constructed-response kinds of test items, there are several general guidelines that, if adhered to, will lead to better assessment procedures. And, because the original Ten Commandments were stated in fairly stern "Thou shall not" form and have proved successful in shaping many folks' behavior, I shall now dish out five general item-writing commandments structured along the same lines. If followed, these commandments won't get you into heaven, but they will make your assessment schemes slightly more divine. All five commandments are presented in the box below. (I had requested the use of stone tablets, but the publisher instantly dismissed such whimsy.)

Five General Item-Writing Commandments

1. Thou shall not provide opaque directions to students regarding how to respond to your assessment instruments.
2. Thou shall not employ ambiguous statements in your assessment items.
3. Thou shall not provide students with unintentional clues regarding appropriate responses.
4. Thou shall not employ complex syntax in your assessment items.
5. Thou shall not use vocabulary that is more advanced than required.

Binary-Choice Items

A *binary-choice item* gives students only two options from which to select. The most common form of binary-choice item is the *true-false item*. Educators have been using true-false tests probably as far back as Socrates. (True or False: Plato was a type of serving-dish used by Greeks for special meals.) Other variations of binary-choice items would be those in which students must choose between yes-no, right-wrong, correct-incorrect, fact-opinion, and so on.

The virtue of binary-choice items is they are typically so terse that students can answer many items in a short time. Therefore, it is possible to cover a large amount of content in a brief assessment session. The greatest weakness of binary-choice items is that, because there are only two options, students have

9

a 50-50 chance of guessing the correct answer even if they don't have the foggiest idea of what's correct. If a large number of binary-choice items are used, however, that weakness tends to evaporate. After all, although students might guess their way correctly through a few binary-choice items, they would need to be extraordinarily lucky to guess their way correctly through 30 such items.

Item-Writing Guidelines for Binary-Choice Items

1. Phrase items so that a superficial analysis by the student suggests a wrong answer.
2. Rarely use negative statements, and never use double negatives.
3. Include only one concept in each statement.
4. Have an approximately equal number of items representing the two categories being tested.
5. Keep item length similar for both categories being tested.

Multiple Binary-Choice Items

A *multiple binary-choice* item is one in which a cluster of items is presented to students, requiring a binary response to each of the items in the cluster. Typically, but not always, the items are related to an initial statement or set of statements. Multiple binary-choice items are formatted so that they look like traditional multiple-choice tests. In a multiple-choice test, the student must choose one answer from several options, but in the multiple binary-choice test the student must make a response for each statement in the cluster.

Research regarding such items suggests that multiple binary-choice items are (1) highly efficient for gathering student achievement data, (2) more reliable than other selected-response items, (3) able to measure the same skills and abilities as multiple-choice items dealing with comparable content, (4) a bit more difficult for students than multiple-choice tests, and (5) perceived by students to be more difficult but more efficient than multiple-choice items. When teachers construct multiple binary-choice items, they must be attentive to all of the usual considerations in writing regular binary-choice items. However, the following two additional guidelines are also important.

Item-Writing Guidelines for Multiple Binary-Choice Items

1. Separate item clusters vividly from one another.
2. Make certain that each item meshes well with the cluster's stimulus material.

Multiple Choice Items

For a number of decades, the *multiple-choice test item* has dominated achievement testing in the United States and many other nations. Multiple-choice items can be used to measure a student's possession of knowledge or a student's ability to engage in higher levels of thinking. A strength of multiple-choice items is they can contain several answers that differ in their relative correctness. Thus, the student can be called on to make subtle distinctions among answer options, several of which may be somewhat correct. A weakness of multiple-choice items, as is the case with all selected-response items, is that students need only recognize a correct answer. They need not generate a correct answer. Although a fair amount of criticism has been heaped on multiple-choice items, particularly in recent years, properly constructed multiple-choice items can tap a rich variety of student skills and knowledge and can thus be a useful tool for classroom assessment.

The first part of a multiple-choice item is referred to as the item's stem. The potential answer options are described as *item alternatives*. Incorrect alternatives are typically referred to as the item's *distractors*. Two common ways of creating multiple-choice items are to use an item stem that is either a direct question or an incomplete statement. With younger students, the direct-question approach is preferable. Using either direct-question stems or incomplete-statement stems, a multiple-choice item can ask students to select either a correct answer or, instead, to select a best answer.

Let's turn now to a consideration of item-writing guidelines for multiple-choice items. Because of the widespread use of multiple-choice items over the past half-century, there are quite a few experience-sired suggestions regarding how to create such items. Below, you'll find five of the more frequently cited recommendations for constructing multiple-choice items.

Item-Writing Guidelines for Multiple-Choice Items

1. The stem should consist of a self-contained question or problem.
2. Avoid negatively stated stems.
3. Do not let the length of alternatives supply unintended clues.
4. Randomly assign correct answers to alternative positions.
5. Never use "all-of-the-above" alternatives, but do use "none-of-the-above" alternatives to increase item difficulty.

Matching Items

A *matching item* consists of two parallel lists of words or phrases that require the student to match entries on one list with appropriate entries on the second list. Entries in the list for which a match is sought are referred to as *premises*.

11

Entries in the list from which selections are made are referred to as *responses*. Usually, students are directed to match entries from the two lists according to a specific kind of association that is described in the test directions.

An advantage of matching items is that their compact form takes up little space on a printed page, thus making it easy to tap a good deal of information efficiently. Matching items can also be easily scored by simply holding a correct-answer template next to the list of premises where students are to supply their selections from the list of responses. A disadvantage of matching items is that, as with binary-choice items, they sometimes encourage students' memorization of low-level factual information that, in at least some instances, is of debatable utility. The illustrative matching item is a case in point. Although it's relatively easy to create matching items such as this, is it really important to know which U.S. chief executive was in office when a military conflict was concluded? That's the kind of issue you'll be facing when you decide what kinds of items to include in your classroom assessments.

Typically, matching items are used as part of a teacher's assessment instruments. It's pretty difficult to imagine a major classroom examination that would consist exclusively of matching items. Matching items don't work well when teachers are trying to assess relatively distinctive ideas, because matching items require pools of related entries to insert into the matching format.

Let's consider a half-dozen guidelines that you should think about when creating matching items for your classroom assessment instruments. The guidelines are presented here.

Item-Writing Guidelines for Matching Items

1. Employ homogeneous lists.
2. Use relatively brief lists, placing the shorter words or phrases at the right.
3. Employ more responses than premises.
4. Order the responses logically.
5. Describe the basis for matching and the number of times responses may be used.

7: Constructed-Response Items

Let's turn, now, to items for classroom assessments that oblige students to construct their own responses rather than choosing their answers from already-presented options. In turn, we'll look at short-answer items and essay items.

Short-Answer Items

The first kind of constructed-response item we'll look at is the *short-answer item*. Short-answer items call for students to supply a word, a phrase, or a sentence in response to either a direct question or an incomplete statement. If an item asks students to come up with a fairly lengthy response, it would be considered an essay item, not a short-answer item. If the item asks students to supply only a single word, then it's a *really* short-answer item.

Short-answer items are suitable for assessing relatively simple kinds of learning outcomes such as those focused on students' acquisition of knowledge. If crafted carefully, however, short-answer items can measure substantially more challenging kinds of learning outcomes. The major advantage of short-answer items is that students need to *produce* a correct answer, not merely recognize it from a set of selected-response options. The level of partial knowledge that might allow a student to respond correctly to a choose-the-best-response item won't be sufficient when the student is required to produce a correct answer to a short-answer item.

The major drawback with short-answer items, as is true with all constructed-response items, is that students' responses are difficult to score. The longer the responses sought, the tougher it is to score them accurately.

Here, you will find five straightforward item-writing guidelines for short-answer items.

Item-Writing Guidelines for Short-Answer Items

1. Usually employ direct questions rather than incomplete statements, particularly for young students.
2. Structure the item so that a response should be concise.
3. Place blanks in the margin for direct questions or near the end of incomplete statements.
4. For incomplete statements, use only one or, at most, two blanks.
5. Make sure blanks for all items are equal in length.

Short-answer items are the most simple form of constructed-response items, but they can help teachers measure important skills and knowledge. Because such items seek students' constructed rather than selected responses, they can be employed to tap some genuinely higher-order skills. Although students' responses to short-answer items are more difficult to score than are their answers to selected-response items, the scoring of such items isn't all that difficult. That's because short-answer items, by definition, should elicit only short answers.

Essay Items: Development

The essay item is surely the most commonly used form of constructed-response assessment item. Any time teachers ask their students to churn out a paragraph or two on what the students know about Topic X or to compose an original composition describing their "Favorite Day," an *essay item* is being used. Essay items are particularly useful in gauging a student's ability to synthesize, evaluate, and compose. Such items have a wide variety of applications in most teachers' classrooms.

A special form of the essay item is the *writing sample*—when teachers ask students to generate a written composition in an attempt to measure students' composition skills. Because the procedures employed to construct items for such writing samples and, thereafter, for scoring students' compositions are so similar to the procedures employed to create and score responses to any kind of essay item, we'll treat writing samples and other kinds of essay items all at one time in this section. You'll find it helpful, however, to remember that the requirement to have students generate a writing sample is, in reality, a widely used type of performance test. We'll dig more deeply into *performance tests* in the following section.

For assessing certain kinds of complex learning outcomes, the essay item is the hands-down winner. It clearly triumphs when you're trying to see how well students can create original compositions. Yet, there are a fair number of drawbacks associated with essay items, and if you're going to consider using essay items in your own classroom, you ought to know the weaknesses as well as the strengths of this item type.

One difficulty with essay items is that they're more difficult to write—at least write properly—than is generally thought. I must confess that as a first-year high school teacher, I sometimes conjured up essay items while walking to school, then slapped them up in the chalkboard so that I created almost instant essay exams. At the time, I thought my essay items were pretty good. Such is the pride of youth and the product of ignorance. I'm glad that I have no record of those items. In retrospect, I assume they were pretty putrid. I now know that generating a really good essay item is a tough task—a task that could not be accomplished while strolling to school. You'll see that's true from the item-writing rules to be presented shortly. It takes time to create a solid essay item. You'll need to find time to construct suitable essay items for your own classroom assessments.

Because the scoring of essay responses (and students' compositions) is such an important topic, you'll soon be getting a separate set of guidelines on how to score responses to such items. The more complex the nature of students' constructed responses become, the more attention you'll need to lavish on scoring. You can't score responses to items that you haven't written, however, so let's look at the five guidelines for the construction of essay items.

Item-Writing Guidelines for Essay Items

1. Convey to students a clear idea regarding the extensiveness of the response desired.
2. Construct items so that the student's task is explicitly described.
3. Provide students with the approximate time to be expended on each item as well as each item's value.
4. Do not employ optional items.
5. Precursively judge an item's quality by composing, mentally or in writing, a possible response.

Here, then, are several guidelines for scoring students' responses to your wonderful essay items.

Guidelines for Scoring Responses to Essay Items

1. Score responses holistically and/or analytically.
2. Prepare a tentative scoring key in advance of judging students' responses.
3. Make decisions regarding the importance of the mechanics of writing prior to scoring.
4. Score all responses to one item before scoring responses to the next item.
5. Insofar as possible, evaluate responses anonymously.

A **holistic scoring** strategy, as its name suggests, focuses on the essay response (or written composition) as a whole. At one extreme of scoring rigor, the teacher can, in a fairly unsystematic manner, supply a "general impression" overall grade to each student's response. Or, in a more systematic fashion, the teacher can isolate, in advance of scoring, those evaluative criteria that should be attended to in order to arrive at a single, overall score per essay. Generally, a score range of four to six points is used for each response. (Some scoring schemes have a few more points, some a few less.) A teacher, then, after

15

considering whatever factors should be attended to in a given item, will give a score to each student's response.

In contrast, an *analytic scoring* scheme strives to be a fine-grained, specific point-allocation approach. Suppose, for example, that instead of using a holistic method of scoring students' compositions, a teacher chose to employ an analytic method of scoring students' compositions. Under those circumstances, a scoring guide must be used by the teacher. For each evaluative criterion in the guide, the teacher must award a certain number of points.

The advantage of an analytic scoring system is that it can help you identify the specific strengths and weaknesses of your students' performances and, therefore, communicate such diagnoses to students in a pinpointed fashion. The downside of analytic scoring is that a teacher sometimes becomes so attentive to the subpoints in a scoring system that, almost literally, the forest (overall quality) can't be seen because of a focus on individual trees (the separate scoring criteria). In less metaphoric language, the teacher will miss the communication of the student's response "as a whole" because of excessive attention to a host of individual evaluative criteria.

One middle-of-the-road scoring approach can be seen when teachers initially grade all students' responses holistically, then return for an analytic scoring of only those responses that were judged, overall, to be unsatisfactory. After the analytic scoring of the unsatisfactory responses, the teacher then relays more fine-grained diagnostic information to those students whose unsatisfactory responses were analytically scored. The idea with this sort of hybrid approach is that the students who are most in need of fine-grained feedback are those who, on the basis of the holistic evaluation, are performing less well.

8: Performance Assessment

During the early 1990s, a good many educational policymakers became enamored with performance assessment. *Performance assessment* is an approach to measuring a student's status based on the way that the student completes a specified task. Theoretically, of course, when the student chooses between true and false for a binary-choice item, the student is completing a task, although an obviously modest one. But the proponents of performance assessment have measurement schemes in mind that are meaningfully different from binary-choice or multiple-choice tests. Indeed, it was a dissatisfaction with traditional paper-and-pencil tests that caused many educators to scurry down the performance-testing trail.

Before digging into what makes performance tests tick and how you might use them in your own classroom, we'd best explore the chief attributes of such an assessment approach. Even though all educational tests, as noted earlier, require students to perform in some way, when most educators talk about performance tests, they are thinking about assessments in which the student is required to construct an original response. More often than not, an examiner (such as the teacher) observes the process of construction so that observation of the student's performance and judgment of that performance are required.

Different educators will often use the phrase *performance assessment* to refer to very different kinds of assessment approaches. Many teachers, for example, are willing to consider short-answer and essay tests a form of performance assessment. In other words, they essentially equate performance assessment with any form of constructed-response assessment. Other teachers establish more stringent requirements in order for a measurement procedure to be described as a performance assessment. For example, some performance assessment proponents contend that genuine performance assessments must possess at least three features:

- *Multiple evaluative criteria.* The student's performance must be judged using more than one evaluative criterion. To illustrate, a student's ability to speak Spanish might be appraised on the basis of the student's accent, syntax, and vocabulary.
- *Prespecified quality standards.* Each of the evaluative criteria on which a student's performance is to be judged is clearly explicated in advance of judging the quality of the student's performance.
- *Judgmental appraisal.* Unlike the scoring of selected-response tests in which electronic computers and scanning machines can, once programmed, carry on without the need of humankind, genuine performance assessments depend on human judgments to determine how acceptable a student's performance really is.

A good many advocates of performance assessment would prefer that the tasks presented to students represent real-world rather than school-world kinds of problems. Other proponents of performance assessment would be elated simply if more school-world measurement was constructed response rather than selected response in nature. Still other advocates of performance testing want the tasks in performance tests to be genuinely *demanding*. In short, proponents of performance assessment often advocate different approaches to measuring students on the basis of how they perform.

You'll sometimes encounter educators who use other phrases to describe performance assessment. For example, they may use the phrase authentic assessment (because the assessment tasks more closely coincide with real-life, nonschool tasks) or alternative assessment (because such assessments constitute an alternative to traditional, paper-and-pencil tests). In the next section, we'll be considering portfolio assessment, which is a particular type of performance assessment and should not be considered a synonymous descriptor for the performance assessment approach to educational measurement.

Performance assessment typically requires students to respond to a small number of more significant tasks rather than respond to a large number of less significant tasks. Thus, rather than answering 50 multiple-choice items on a conventional chemistry examination, students who are being assessed via performance tasks may find themselves asked to perform an actual experiment in their chemistry class, then write an interpretation of the experiment's results and an analytic critique of the procedures they used. From the chemistry teacher's perspective, instead of seeing how students respond to the 50 "mini-tasks" represented in the multiple-choice test, an estimate of each student's status must be derived from a student's response to a single, complex task. Given the significance of each task that is used in a performance-testing approach to classroom assessment, it is apparent that great care must be taken in the selection of *performance-assessment tasks*. Generally speaking, classroom teachers will either have to (1) generate their own performance test tasks or (2) select performance test tasks from the increasing number of tasks that are available from educators elsewhere.

The scoring procedures for judging students' responses to performance tests are usually referred to these days as *scoring rubrics* or, more simply, *rubrics*. A rubric that's used to score students' responses to a performance assessment has, at minimum, three important features:

- *Evaluative criteria.* These are the factors to be used in determining the quality of a student's response.
- *Descriptions of qualitative differences for the evaluative criteria.* For each evaluative criterion, a description must be supplied so that qualitative distinctions in students' responses can be made using the criterion.

- *An indication of whether a holistic or analytic scoring approach is to be used.* The rubric must indicate whether the evaluative criteria are to be applied collectively in the form of *holistic* scoring or on a criterion-by-criterion basis in the form of *analytic* scoring.

The identification of a rubric's evaluative criteria, as might be guessed, is probably the most important task for rubric developers. If you're creating a rubric for a performance test that you wish to use in your own classroom, be careful not to come up with a lengthy laundry list of the evaluative criteria a student's response should satisfy. Personally, I think that when you isolate more than three or four evaluative criteria per rubric, you've identified too many. If you find yourself facing more than a few evaluative criteria, simply *rank each criterion in order of importance*, then chop off those listed lower than three or four.

The next job you'll have is deciding how to *describe in words* what a student's response must be in order to be judged wonderful or woeful. The level of descriptive detail that you apply needs to work *for you*. Remember, you're devising a scoring rubric for your own classroom, not a statewide or national test. Keep the aversiveness of the work down by employing brief descriptors of quality differences that you can use and, if you're instructionally astute, your students can use as well.

Finally, you'll need to decide whether you'll make a single, overall judgment about a student's response by considering all of the rubric's evaluative criteria (holistic scoring) or, instead, award the response points on a criterion-by-criterion basis (analytic scoring). The virtue of holistic scoring, of course, is that it's quicker to do. The downside of holistic scoring is that it fails to communicate to students, especially low-performing students, what their shortcomings are. Clearly, analytic scoring yields a greater likelihood of diagnostically pinpointed scoring and sensitive feedback than does holistic scoring. Some classroom teachers have attempted to garner the best of both worlds by scoring all responses holistically, then analytically rescoring (for feedback purposes) all responses of low-performing students.

Performance assessment has been around for a long, long while. Yet, in recent years, a growing number of educators have become strong supporters of this form of assessment because it (1) represents an alternative to traditional paper-and-pencil tests and (2) is often more authentic—that is, reflective of tasks that people need to perform in the real world. One of the things you need to understand about performance assessment is that it differs from more conventional assessment chiefly in the degree the assessment task matches the behavior domain to which you wish to make inferences. Because performance tasks coincide more closely with such domains than do paper-and-pencil tests, more accurate inferences can often be derived about students. Another big plus for performance tests is they establish assessment targets that, because such targets often influence the teacher's instruction, have a positive impact on instructional activities.

You need to realize, however, that because performance tasks require a fair chunk of time from students, the teacher is often faced with making rather shaky generalizations on the basis of relatively few student performances. It's also important for you to recognize that the development of defensible performance tests is difficult cerebral work. It takes rigorous thinking to identify suitable tasks for performance tests, then isolate appropriate evaluative criteria and spell out the scoring scale for each criterion. And, of course, once the test and its associated scoring procedures are in place, you still have to score students' performances, an operation that invariably takes much more time than is required to score a ream of answers to selected-response items.

9: Portfolio Assessment

"Assessment should be a part of instruction, not apart from it" is a point of view that most proponents of portfolio assessment would enthusiastically endorse. Portfolio assessment, a relatively recent entry in the educational measurement derby, has captured the attention of large numbers of educators because it represents a clear alternative to more traditional forms of educational testing.

A *portfolio* is a systematic collection of one's work. In education, portfolios refer to systematic collections of students' work. Although the application of portfolios in education has been a relatively recent phenomenon, portfolios have been widely used in a number of other fields for many years. Portfolios, in fact, constitute the chief method by which certain professionals display their skills and accomplishments. For example, portfolios are traditionally used for that purpose by photographers, artists, journalists, models, architects, and so on. An important feature of portfolios is that they must be updated as a person's achievements and skills grow. Portfolios have been warmly embraced by those educators who regard traditional assessment with less than enthusiasm.

Although there are numerous ways to install and sustain portfolios in a classroom, you will find that the following seven-step sequence provides a reasonable template for getting underway with portfolio assessment. Taken together, these seven activities capture the key ingredients in classroom-based portfolio assessment.

1. *Make sure your students "own" their portfolios.* In order for portfolios to represent a student's evolving work accurately, and to foster the kind of self-evaluation that is so crucial if portfolios are to be truly educational, students must perceive portfolios to be collections of their own work and not merely temporary receptacles for products that you ultimately grade. You will probably want to introduce the notion of portfolio assessment to your students (assuming that portfolio assessment isn't already a schoolwide operation and that your students aren't already familiar with the use of portfolios) by explaining the distinctive functions of portfolios in the classroom.

2. *Decide on what kinds of work samples to collect.* Various kinds of work samples can be included in a portfolio. Obviously, such products will vary from subject to subject. In general, a wide variety of work products is preferable to a limited range of work products. Ideally, you and your students can collaboratively determine what goes in the portfolio.

3. *Collect and store work samples.* Students need to collect the designated work samples as they are created, place them in a suitable container (a folder or notebook, for example), then store the container

21

in a file cabinet, storage box, or some suitably safe location. You may need to work individually with your students to help them decide whether particular products should be placed in their portfolios. The actual organization of a portfolio's contents depends, of course, on the nature of the work samples being collected.

4. *Select criteria by which to evaluate portfolio work samples.* Working collaboratively with students, carve out a set of criteria by which you and your students can judge the quality of their portfolio products. Because of the likely diversity of products in different students' portfolios, the identification of evaluative criteria will not be a simple task. Yet, unless at least rudimentary evaluative criteria are isolated, the students will find it difficult to evaluate their own efforts and, thereafter, to strive for improvement. The criteria, once selected, should be described with the same sort of clarity we saw in the previous chapter regarding how to use rubrics when evaluating students' responses to performance test tasks.

5. *Require students to evaluate continually their own portfolio products.* Using the agreed-on criteria, be sure that your students try to evaluate their own work. Students can be directed to evaluate their work products holistically, analytically, or using a combination of both approaches. Such self-evaluation can be made routine by requiring each student to complete brief evaluation slips on 3" ʹ 5" cards on which they identify the major strengths and weaknesses of a given product, then suggest how the product could be improved. Be sure to have your students date such self-evaluation sheets so they can keep track of modifications in their self-evaluation skills. Each completed self-evaluation sheet should be stapled or paper-clipped to the work product being evaluated.

6. *Schedule and conduct portfolio conferences.* Portfolio conferences take time. Yet, these interchange sessions between teachers and students regarding students' work are really pivotal in making sure that portfolio assessment fulfills its potential. The conference should not only evaluate your students' work products but should also help them improve their self-evaluation abilities. Try to hold as many of these conferences as you can. In order to make the conferences time efficient, be sure to have students prepare for the conferences so that you can start right in on the topics of most concern to you and the student.

7. *Involve parents in the portfolio assessment process.* Early in the school year, make sure your students' parents understand what the nature of the portfolio assessment process is that you've devised for your classroom. Insofar as is practical, encourage your students' parents/guardians periodically to review their children's work samples

as well as their children's self-evaluation of those work samples. The more active that parents become in reviewing their children's work, the stronger the message will be to the child that the portfolio activity is really worthwhile. If you wish, you may have students select their best work for a showcase portfolio or, instead, simply use the students' working portfolios.

These seven steps reflect only the most important activities that teachers might engage in when creating assessment programs in their classrooms. There are obviously all sorts of variations and embellishments that are possible.

As noted at the beginning to this four-section excursion into item types, the more familiar that you are with different kinds of test items, the more likely you will be to select an item type that best provides you with the information you need in order to draw suitable inferences about your students. Until recently, portfolios haven't been viewed as a viable assessment option by many teachers. These days, however, portfolio assessment clearly is a legitimate contender in the measurement derby.

You need to realize that if portfolio assessment is going to constitute a helpful adjunct to your instructional program, portfolios will have to become a central, not tangential, part of what goes on in your classroom. The primary premise in portfolio assessment is that a particularized collection of a student's *evolving* work will allow both the student and you to determine the student's progress. You can't gauge the student's evolving progress if you don't have frequent evidence of the student's efforts.

It would probably be educationally unwise to select portfolio assessment as a one-time measurement approach to deal with a short-term instructional objective. Rather, it makes more sense to select some goal of interest, such as the student's ability to write original compositions, then monitor that aspect of the student's learning throughout the entire school year. It is also important for you to realize that although portfolio assessment may prove highly valuable for classroom instruction and measurement purposes, at this juncture there is insufficient evidence that it can be used appropriately for large-scale assessment.

A number of portfolio assessment specialists believe that the most important dividend from portfolio assessment is the increased abilities of students to evaluate their own work. If this becomes one of your goals in a portfolio assessment approach, you must be certain to nurture such self-evaluation growth deliberately via portfolios instead of simply using portfolios as convenient collections of work samples for you to appraise.

The seven key ingredients in portfolio assessment that were just identified represent only one way of installing this kind of assessment strategy. Variations of those seven suggested procedures are not only possible, but to be encouraged. The big thing to keep in mind is that portfolio assessment offers your students and you a way to particularize your evaluation of each student's growth over time. And, speaking of time, it's only appropriate to remind you that it takes substantially more time to use a portfolio assessment approach properly than to score a zillion true-false tests. If you opt to try portfolio assessment, you'll have to see whether, in your own instructional situation, it yields sufficient educational benefits to be worth the investment you'll surely need to make in it.

10: Affective Assessment

Affective variables, most educators concede, are important. Students' attitudes toward learning, for example, play a major role in how much learning those students subsequently pursue. The values that students have regarding truthfulness and integrity shape their daily conduct. And students' self-esteem, of course, influences almost everything they do. There's little doubt that the affective status of students should concern all educators.

In truth, however, few classroom teachers give explicit attention to influencing their students' attitudes and values. Even fewer classroom teachers actually try to assess the affective status of their students. Certainly, a teacher may observe a student's sour demeanor and conclude that he's "out of sorts" or she's "a mite depressed," but how many times have you heard about a teacher who tried to gather *systematic* evidence regarding students' attitudes and values? Unfortunately, systematic assessment of affect is pretty uncommon.

One question you might be asking yourself is, Why assess attitudes at all? Many teachers, particularly those who teach older students, believe that their only educational mission is to increase students' knowledge and skills. Affect, such teachers believe, simply doesn't fall into their proper sphere of influence. However, students who learn to do mathematics like magicians yet abhor mathematics certainly aren't apt to apply the mathematics they've learned. Students who can compose outstanding essays but believe they are "really rotten writers" won't spend much time volitionally whipping out essays.

I'd like to get my own bias regarding this issue out on the table so you don't think I'm trying to subliminally influence you. I personally regard affective variables as far more significant than cognitive variables. How many times, for example, have you seen people who weren't all that "gifted" intellectually still succeed because they were highly motivated and hard working? Conversely, how many times have you seen truly able people simply veer away from challenges because they did not consider themselves worthy? Day in and day out, we see the enormous impact that people's affective status has on them. Affect is every bit as important as cognitive ability.

Have you ever seen a group of kindergarten students troop off to school loaded with enthusiasm and gumption, only to encounter those same students a few years later and see that a fair number were disenchanted with school and down on themselves? Well, I have. And what's going on with such children is surely taking place in the affective realm. When most kindergartners start school, they are enthused about school and themselves. However, after failing to measure up for a year or two, many of those formerly upbeat children carry around decisively lowered self-concepts. They've tried and been found wanting. Such negative attitudes about self and school will typically influence all of a child's subsequent education. Yet, because few teachers try to assess their students' affective status, most teachers don't know what their students' attitudes and values really are. That situation, I believe, needs to change.

Even if there were no such thing as externally imposed "educational accountability" whereby students' performances on high-stakes tests serve as indicators of educational effectiveness, what's on achievement tests would still influence what teachers teach. When I was a high school teacher, I knew what kinds of items I had on my final exams. (That is, I knew in the second year of teaching, after I'd whipped out my first-year final exams only minutes before my students needed to take those exams.) Because I wanted my students to do well on my final exams, I made reasonably sure that I spent at least some instructional time on the content covered by the final examinations.

It's the same with affective assessment. Let's say you've installed a fairly straightforward pretest-posttest evaluation design to assess any meaningful changes in your students' responses to an attitude inventory regarding how much they are interested in the subject(s) you're teaching. Your recognition that there will be a formal pretest-posttest assessment of students' subject-matter interest will, as surely as school buses run late, influence you to provide instruction so that your students will, in fact, become more positive about the subject(s) you're teaching.

In other words, the presence of affective postinstruction measurement will incline you to include affectively focused activities in your instruction. In a sense, you're saying to yourself—and anyone else you care to have understand your instructional planning—that affective outcomes are important enough for you to formally assess. You can be assured that what's important enough to be assessed, even if it's measured in your classroom and nowhere else in the world, is likely to influence your instruction. As I confessed earlier, I think that affectively focused instruction deals with the kinds of outcomes that are the most important we teach.

It has been said that *we measure what we treasure*. Well, if we really think affective outcomes are worth promoting, we darn well ought to measure them.

11: Improving Teacher-Developed Assessments

If you've ever visited the manuscript room of the British Museum, you'll recall seeing handwritten manuscripts authored by some of the superstars of English literature. It's a moving experience. Delightfully, the museum presents not only the final versions of famed works by such authors as Milton and Keats but also the early drafts of those works. It is somewhat surprising and genuinely encouraging to learn that those giants of literature didn't get it right the first time. They had to cross out words, delete sentences, and substitute phrases. Many of the museum's early drafts are genuinely messy, reflecting all sorts of rethinking on the part of the author. Well, if the titans of English literature had to revise their early drafts, is it at all surprising that teachers usually need to spruce up their classroom assessments?

This section is designed to provide you with several procedures by which you can improve the assessment instruments you develop. Although I can promise you that if you use the section's recommended procedures, your tests will get better, they'll probably never make it to the British Museum—unless you carry them in when visiting.

There are two general improvement strategies to be described in this chapter. First, you'll learn about *judgmental item improvement* procedures in which the chief means of sharpening your tests is human judgment—your own and that of others. Second, you'll be considering *empirical item improvement* procedures that are based on students' responses to your assessment procedures. Ideally, if time permits and your motivation abounds, you can use both forms of test-improvement procedures for your own classroom assessment devices.

Human judgment, although it sometimes gets us in trouble, is a remarkably useful tool. Judgmental approaches to test improvement can be carried out quite systematically or, in contrast, rather informally. Judgmental assessment-improvement strategies differ chiefly according to who is supplying the judgments. There are three sources of test-improvement judgments you should consider—those supplied by (1) yourself, (2) your colleagues, and (3) your students. Presented here are five review criteria that you might wish to consider if you set out systematically to improve your classroom assessment procedures:

- *Adherence to item-specific guidelines and general item-writing commandments.* When you review your assessment procedures, it will be useful to review briefly the general item-writing commandments supplied earlier as well as the particular item-writing guidelines provided for the specific kind of item(s) you've developed. If you now see violations of the principles set forth in either of those two sets of directives, fix the flaws.

27

- *Contribution to score-based inference.* Recall that the real reason teachers assess students is in order to arrive at score-based inferences about the status of students. Therefore, it will be helpful for you to reconsider each aspect of a previously developed assessment procedure to see whether it does, in fact, really contribute to the kind of inference about your students that you wish to draw.

- *Accuracy of content.* There's always the possibility that previously accurate content has now been superseded or contradicted by more recent content. Be sure to check that the content you included earlier in the assessment instrument is still accurate and that your answer key is still correct.

- *Absence of content lacunae.* This review criterion gives me a chance to use one of my favorite words, the plural form of *lacuna,* which, incidentally, means a *gap.* Although *gap* would have done the job in this instance, you'll admit that gap looks somewhat tawdry when stacked up against *lacuna.* Hindsight is a nifty form of vision. Thus, when you take a second look at the content coverage represented in your assessment instrument, you may discover that you originally overlooked some important content. This review criterion is clearly related to an earlier review criterion regarding the assessment's contribution to the score-based inference that you want to make. Any meaningful lacunae in content will obviously reduce the accuracy of your inference.

- *Fairness.* Although you should clearly have tried to eradicate any bias in your assessment instruments when you originally developed them, there's always the chance that you overlooked something. Undertake another bias review just to make certain you've been as attentive to bias elimination as you possibly can be.

In addition to judgmentally based methods of improving your assessment procedures, there are improvement approaches based on the empirical data that students supply when they respond to the assessment instruments you've developed. A variety of empirical item-improvement techniques have been well honed over the years. For example, you can look at how difficult an item is, based on the proportion of your students who answer the item correctly. Or you might determine *which* students answer an item correctly, that is, the student who score well or poorly on the entire test. All of these empirical item-improvement indices are explained in most educational measurement textbooks.

12: Instructionally Oriented Assessment

Teachers test a child in order to make better decisions about how to educate the child. At least, they ought to.

In this section, I'm going to describe two ways that the quality of a teacher's instruction can be markedly improved as a consequence of classroom assessments. One of those assessment-based strategies for improving instruction is fairly well known by teachers—even if it's not all that widely employed. The second assessment-based strategy for improving instruction, on the other hand, is understood by relatively few teachers.

The two assessment-based strategies for instructional improvement that will be the focus of this chapter are presented below:

Strategy One: Making instructional decisions in light of assessment results. A teacher makes instructional decisions after assessing students to determine their status regarding the teacher's educational objectives.

Strategy Two: Planning instruction to achieve the objective(s) represented by a test. A teacher deliberately designs instruction to promote students' attainment of the knowledge, skills, and/or affect exemplified by an assessment.

Let's now briefly consider each of these two ways of strengthening instruction.

If teachers accept the proposition that students' performances on assessments should inform a teacher's instructional decisions, they'll usually discover there are three major categories of decisions that can be made better if students' assessment performances are considered. Those three kinds of instructional decisions are listed in Table 12.1.

Because of the heightened attention to student performance on important statewide and district-wide tests, we also see clearly identifiable attention being given to the evidence of student success on teacher-made *classroom* tests. Many educational administrators and policymakers have concluded that if students' performances on statewide tests reflect a school's educational effectiveness, then even at the classroom level, good test results indicate that good teaching is taking place, while bad test results indicate the opposite. Greater and greater emphasis is being given to "evidence of effectiveness" in the form of improved student performance on whatever types of classroom tests are being employed. Increasingly, *evidence* of student learning—evidence in the form of student performance on classroom tests—is being used in the personnel appraisals of teachers. Teachers' competence is being determined, at least in part, by how well a teacher's students perform on the teacher's classroom tests.

Table 12.1 Categories of Instructional Decisions Enhanced by a Consideration of Students' Assessment Performances

Decision Category	Typical Assessment Strategy	Decision Options
• What to teach in the first place?	Preassessment prior to the start of instruction	Whether to provide instruction for specific instructional objectives?
• How long to keep teaching toward a particular instructional objective?	En route assessments of students' progress	Whether to continue or cease instruction for an objective, either for an individual student or for the whole class?
• How effective was an instructional sequence?	Comparing students' posttest to pretest performances	Whether to retain, discard, or modify a given instructional sequence the next time it's used?

Given this ever-increasing administrative reliance on student test results as one indicator of a teacher's instructional effectiveness, it is only natural that many teachers tried to address instructionally whatever was to be tested. Tests had clearly begun to influence teaching. And it was increasingly recognized by teachers not only that the content of their tests *could* influence their teaching but, perhaps, the content of those tests *should* influence their teaching.

If testing should influence teaching, why not construct classroom assessments *prior* to instructional planning? In that way, any planned instructional sequence could mesh more effectively with the content of the test involved. Moreover, why not build classroom assessments with the instructional implications of those assessments deliberately in mind? In other words, why not build a classroom assessment not only before any instructional planning, but in such a way that the assessment would beneficially inform the teacher's instructional planning? Such an approach, as you might have already guessed, is the essence of the second assessment-based strategy to improve instructional quality. A contrast between a more traditional educational approach in which instruction influences assessment and the kind of assessment-influenced instruction being described here can be seen in Figure 12.1.

In a traditional approach to instructional design, an approach in which instruction influences assessment, the teacher (1) is guided by the curriculum that's been adopted by the state and/or district, (2) plans instructional activities to promote the educational objectives set forth in that curriculum, and (3) assesses students. In an assessment-influenced approach to instructional design, also indicated in Figure 12.1, the teacher still (1) starts with the educational objectives set forth in the curriculum, (2) then moves to create assessments based on those goals, and (3) only thereafter plans instructional activities intended to promote students' mastery of the knowledge, skills, and/or attitudes that are to be assessed. In both approaches, curriculum is the starting point. Educational objectives, or content standards, still govern the entire process. But in the two contrasting approaches, the sequence of instructional planning and assessment development is reversed.

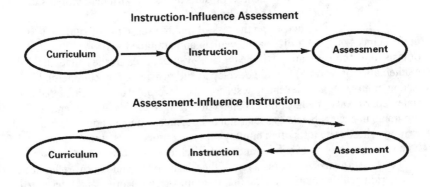

Figure 12.1 **Traditional Instruction-Influenced Assessment versus Assessment-Influenced Instruction, Both of Which Are Governed by Curricular Considerations**

31

13:   Making Sense Out of Standardized Test Scores

Classroom teachers need to be able to interpret the results not only of their own assessment procedures but also of the various kinds of standardized tests that are frequently administered to students. Teachers need to be able to interpret such test results so they can base classroom instructional decisions on those results and also be able to respond accurately when students' parents raise such questions as, "What does my child's grade-equivalent score of 7.4 really mean?" or "When my child's achievement test results are at the 97th percentile, is that three percentiles from the top or the bottom?"

This section focuses on the task of making sense out of students' performances on standardized achievement and aptitude tests. One of the kinds of tests under consideration will be the achievement tests (for instance, in mathematics or reading) that are developed and distributed by commercial testing companies. Achievement tests are also developed and administered by state departments of education in connection with statewide assessment programs in such subjects as social studies, sciences, mathematics, reading, and writing. These state tests often employ reporting procedures akin to those used with commercially distributed standardized achievement tests.

A *standardized test* is a test, either designed to yield norm-referenced or criterion-referenced inferences, that is administered, scored, and interpreted in a standard manner. Almost all *nationally* standardized tests are distributed by commercial testing firms. Most such firms are for-profit corporations, although there are a few not-for-profit measurement organizations, such as the Educational Testing Service (ETS), that distribute nationally standardized tests. Almost all nationally standardized tests, whether focused on the measurement of students' aptitude or achievement, are chiefly intended to provide norm-referenced interpretations.

Standardized achievement tests have also been developed in a number of states under the auspices of state departments of education. These statewide tests (clearly intended to be administered, scored, and interpreted in a standardized fashion) have usually been installed to satisfy a legislative mandate aimed at achieving a form of educational accountability. In some instances, important decisions about individual students are made on the basis of a student's test performance. In many states, for example, if a student does not pass a prescribed statewide basic skills examination by the end of high school, the student is not awarded a diploma, even though all other curricular requirements have been satisfied. In other cases, even though no contingencies for individual students depend on how a student performed on a test, results of student tests are publicized on a district-by-district or school-by-school basis. The test results thus serve as an indicator of local educators' effectiveness, at least in the perception of many citizens. These state-sired standardized achievement tests are generally intended to yield criterion-referenced interpretations. Educational aptitude tests are not developed by state departments of education.

Although standardized tests have traditionally consisted almost exclusively of selected-response items, in recent years the developers of standardized tests have attempted to incorporate an increasing number of constructed-response items in their tests. Standardized tests, because they are intended for widespread use, are developed with far more care (and cost) than is possible in an individual teacher's classroom. Even so, the fundamentals of test development that you've learned about in earlier chapters are routinely employed when standardized tests are developed. In other words, the people who create the items for such tests attempt to adhere to the same kinds of item-writing and item-improvement precepts you've learned about. The writers of multiple-choice items for standardized tests worry, just as you should, about inadvertently supplying examinees with clues that give away the correct answer. The writers of short-answer items for standardized tests try to avoid, just as you should, the inclusion of ambiguous language in their items.

There are, of course, staggering differences in the level of effort associated with the construction of standardized tests and the construction of classroom tests. a commercial testing agency may assign a fleet of item writers and a flock of item editors to a new test-development project, whereas you'll be fortunate if you have a part-time teacher's aide or, possibly, a malleable spouse to proofread your tests to see if there are typographical errors.

Because results of standardized tests are almost certain to come into your professional life, at least in some form, you need to have an intuitive understanding of how to interpret those results. The most common ways of describing a set of scores is to provide an index of the score distribution's central tendency (usually the mean or median) and an index of the score distribution's variability (usually the standard deviation or the range). There will probably be instances in which you either have to describe the performances of your students or to understand the descriptions of the performances of other groups of students (such as all students in your school or your district).

To make accurate interpretations of standardized test scores for your own students, and to help parents understand how to make sense of their child's standardized test scores, you need to comprehend the basic meaning of percentiles, grade-equivalent scores, and scale scores. You really ought to know what the major advantage and disadvantage of each of those three score-interpretation schemes is. You'll then be in a position to help parents make sense out of their children's performances on standardized tests.

14: Appropriate and Inappropriate Test-Preparation Practices

This section deals with an important assessment-related issue that never really troubled teachers a decade or two ago. Unfortunately, it is a problem that today's classroom teachers have to confront seriously. Faced with growing pressures to increase students' scores on achievement tests, some teachers have responded by engaging in test-preparation practices that are highly questionable. In recent years, for example, a number of reports have been made of teachers and administrators who deliberately coached students with actual copies of a supposedly "secure" examination. There are even reports of educators' erasing students' incorrect answers and substituting correct answers in their place. Teachers caught cheating on high-stakes tests have lost both their teaching licenses and their jobs. Rather than a few isolated instances, such violations of test security are becoming, sadly, quite common.

Two Evaluative Guidelines

Two guidelines can be employed by teachers who wish to ascertain the appropriateness of given test-preparation practices. Taken together, the two guidelines provide teachers with advice regarding the suitability of particular test-preparation activities. Here, then, is the first guideline—*the professional ethics guideline*.

Professional Ethics

No test-preparation practice should violate the ethical norms of the education profession.

This first guideline obliges teachers to avoid any test-preparation practice that is unethical. Ethical behaviors, of course, are rooted not only in fundamental morality but also in the nature of a particular profession. For example, physicians should be governed by general ethical principles dealing with honesty and respect for other people's property as well as by ethical principles that have evolved specifically for the medical profession. Similarly, teachers should not engage in test-preparation practices that involve violations of general ethical canons dealing with theft, cheating, lying, and so on. In addition, however, teachers must take seriously the ethical obligations that they undertake because they have agreed to serve *in loco parentis*. Teachers who serve "in place of the parent" take on an ethical responsibility to serve as models of ethical behavior for children.

It should also be noted that when teachers engage in test-preparation practices that, if brought to the public's attention, would discredit the education profession, such practices may be considered professionally unethical. This is because, in the long term, such practices erode public confidence in our schools and, as a result, financial support for the schools. Consequently, this erosion of public support renders the education profession less potent.

Thus, according to the guideline of professional ethics, teachers should not engage in test-preparation practices that involve such behaviors as violating state-imposed security procedures regarding high-stakes tests. A growing number of states have enacted serious and widely promulgated regulations so that teachers who breach state test-security procedures can have their credentials revoked. Accordingly, teachers should not engage in test-preparation practices that are unethical because there are potential personal repercussions (for example, loss of credentials) or professional repercussions (for example, reduced citizen confidence in public schooling). Most importantly, teachers should avoid unethical test-preparation practices because such practices are *wrong*.

Let's look, then, at the second of our two guidelines—*the educational defensibility guideline*.

Educational Defensibility

No test-preparation practice should increase students' test scores without simultaneously increasing students' mastery of the assessment domain tested.

This second standard emphasizes the importance of engaging in instructional practices that are in the educational best interests of students. Teachers should not, for example, artificially increase students' scores on a test while neglecting to increase students' mastery of the domain of knowledge and/or skills that the test is supposed to reflect.

The result of such inappropriate test-preparation practices is that a deceptive picture of students' achievement is created. The test results no longer serve as an accurate indicator of students' status with respect to an assessment domain. As a consequence, students who in reality have not mastered a domain of content may fail to receive appropriate instruction regarding such content. The students will have been instructionally shortchanged because inappropriate test-preparation practices led to an inflated estimate of their content mastery. Such test-preparation practices, because they rob students of needed instruction, are educationally indefensible.

If you get into any sort of meaningful discussion of test preparation, it's almost certain that someone will soon use the expression "teaching to the test." That someone should not be you! Here's why.

There are two decisively different meanings that people employ when they use the phrase *teaching to the test*. First, they can mean that a teacher is directing instruction toward the knowledge, skills, or affective variables represented by the test. Another way to put this first meaning of "teaching to the test" is that teachers are aiming their instruction so that students accomplish the assessment domain sampled by the actual test. This is good instruction. A second meaning of "teaching to the test" is that it describes teachers who are directing their instruction specifically toward the actual items on the test itself. This is bad instruction.

So, when someone uses the expression "teaching to the test," we can't tell whether they're talking about something swell or something sordid. Conversations that take place about test preparation in which this double-meaning expression is tossed around mindlessly will, almost certainly, end up being mindless conversations.

As a consequence, I implore you *never to use this ambiguous expression* yourself. Rather, say either "teaching to the test's items" or "teaching to the content represented by the test." To emphasize the importance of this advice, I have summarized it below:

NEVER, NEVER SAY:
"Teaching to the test"
SAY:
"Teaching to the test's items"
(or)
SAY:
"Teaching to the content represented by the test"

15: Evaluating Teaching and Grading Students

Evaluation is an activity focused on determining the effectiveness of the teacher, while *grading* is an activity focused on letting students know how well they are performing. *Formative evaluation* can be contrasted with *summative evaluation*. Formative evaluation focuses on the improvement of the teacher's instructional endeavors, whereas summative evaluation focuses on such decisions as continuation of the teacher's employment. A preinstruction versus postinstruction approach is one straightforward way of employing assessment results to help determine the effectiveness of instruction. However, care must be taken in how the pretest and posttest data are collected and then scored.

The inappropriateness of using students' scores on standardized achievement tests occurs because of three chief reasons: (1) mismatches between what's tested and what's taught; (2) a technical tendency to exclude from test items covering important, teacher-stressed content; and (3) uncertainty about the extent to which students' scores are attributable to (a) what has been learned in school, (b) students' socioeconomic backgrounds, or (c) inherited academic aptitudes. Because the use of standardized achievement tests to evaluate schools is likely to yield inaccurate conclusions about instructional quality, teachers are urged to (1) collect more credible evidence of their instructional effectiveness and (2) inform parents and educational policymakers about the need to secure defensible evidence of a teacher's instructional success.

Turning to grading of students, it is recommended that teachers explicate their grading criteria and assign weights to each criterion. Four schemes for arriving at grades are: ability grading, relative grading, aptitude-based grading, and pass/fail grading.

If there ever were two education-related activities in which the results of student assessments play a vital role, those two activities are the evaluation of one's teaching and the grading of one's students. When teachers evaluate the quality of their own efforts, a significant source of data should be the nature of students' performances on classroom assessment devices. When teachers give grades to students, a salient factor should be the quality of students' performances on classroom assessments.

You should realize that when you use students' test results as indicators of your own instructional prowess, a major determiner of how well your students perform will be the particular students with whom you're working. Even using a straightforward pretest-posttest evaluation model doesn't circumvent the problem created because of the dissimilarity of different teachers' students. For purposes of formative evaluation, disparities in students' entry behaviors don't pose all that much of a problem. For purposes of summative evaluation, however, disparities in the abilities and motivation levels of different teachers' students should induce caution in the evaluative use of students' test results. Judgments about the caliber of growth attained by a given teacher must be made in the context of the particular instructional situation in which the teacher is functioning. A particularly useful way of collecting evidence regarding a teacher's instructional effectiveness is the split-and-switch design.

Perhaps one of the most important understandings that you should carry from this section is the recognition that traditional standardized achievement tests—the kind being used all over the land for purposes of educational accountability—should not be employed to evaluate a teacher's instructional effectiveness. You need to understand why such tests are inappropriate for that purpose. And once you recognize *why* the evidence derived from standardized achievement tests is unsuitable for the evaluation of a school staff's quality, then you should see that other evidence, more defensible and more credible, needs to be collected by educators. The public has a right to see how well their tax-supported schools are doing. The public doesn't have the right to do so by using the wrong evidence.

Regarding grading, you should know that you need to give careful attention to the isolation of grading criteria and to the weighting of those criteria. However, when you get down to it—that is, when you get down to the dispensing of actual grades—you're more than likely to miss on certain students. Yet, given the inescapably judgmental basis of grading, that's as good as it's going to get.